_____

_To_

_____

From

Heart
Impressions

Every single act of love bears
the imprint of God.

Gifts of Beauty for Your Soul

Artwork © 2001 Lea Murphy, Whiny Dog Press

www.whinydogpress.com

Text © 2001 Garborg's

Published by Garborg's

P. O. Box 20132, Bloomington, MN 55420

Design by Franke Design

Non-attributed passages written by Wendy Greenberg

Scripture quotations marked NIV are taken from the Holy Bible, New International Version®. Copyright © 1973, 1978, 1984 by International Bible Society. Used by permission of Zondervan Publishing House. Scripture quotations marked MSG are taken from The Message. Copyright © 1993, 1994, 1995, 1996. Used by permission of NavPress Publishing Group. Scripture quotations marked TLB are taken from The Living Bible © 1971. Used by permission of Tyndale House Publishers, Inc., Wheaton, Illinois 60189. All rights reserved.

ISBN 1-58375-897-6

Gifts of Beauty

for Your Soul

Filtering through the leaves, morning light
awakens the day. The dew shimmers
on the sun-dappled ground.
In the stillness of early day, God's presence
lingers in the soft cool air. The stone path
leads to the far corner of the garden
where the roses bloom. Their perfumed
scent inspires the wonder of a new day—
gifts of beauty for the soul.

The steadfast love of the Lord never ceases,
his mercies never come to an end; they are new every morning.

LAMENTATIONS 3:22-23 NRSV

*Y*ou must have a room or
a certain hour of the
day or so where you do not
know what was in the morning paper...
a place where you can simply
experience and bring forth
what you are, and what you might be....
At first you may find nothing's
happening.... But if you have a sacred
place and use it, take advantage
of it, something will happen.

JOSEPH CAMPBELL

*G*od still draws near to us in the ordinary,
commonplace, everyday experiences
and places.... He comes in surprising ways.

HENRY GARIEPY

*F*riendship is the fruit gathered from the trees planted in the rich soil of love, and nurtured with tender care and understanding.

ALMA L. WEIXELBAUM

Friendship is a slow ripening fruit.

ARISTOTLE

FRIENDS ARE LIKE WINDOWS THROUGH

Friends are like

WHICH YOU SEE OUT INTO THE WORLD

windows through which

AND BACK INTO YOURSELF. FRIENDS

you see out into the

windows through which

DOWS THROUGH WHICH YOU SEE OUT

you see out into the

INTO THE WORLD AND BACK INTO

world and back into

YOURSELF. FRIENDS ARE LIKE

The sacred in the ordinary. How can there be
anything sacred in such an ordinary day?
Washing clothes and hanging them out to dry
becomes holy when we breathe in the fresh
summer air, simply grateful to be here.
Doing the dishes becomes a blessed sacrament
when our hearts well up with the gladness
of having just shared a meal with the ones we love.
There is really nothing ordinary about today or any day.

Just to be is a blessing.
Just to live is holy.

ABRAHAM HESCHEL

See, the grass is full of stars,
Fallen in their brightness;
Hearts they have of shining gold,
Rays of shining whiteness.

Buttercups have honeyed hearts,
Bees they love the clover,
But I love the daisies' dance
All the meadow over.

Blow, O blow, you happy winds,
Singing summer's praises,
Up the field and down the field
A-dancing with the daisies.

MARJORIE PICKTHALL

I wandered lonely as a cloud
That floats on high o'er vales and hills,
When all at once I saw a crowd,
A host of golden daffodils,
Beside the lake, beneath the trees
Fluttering and dancing in the breeze.

Continuous as the stars that shine
And twinkle on the milky way,
They stretched in never-ending line
Along the margin of a bay:
Ten thousand saw I at a glance
Tossing their heads in sprightly dance....

For oft, when on my couch I lie
In vacant or in pensive mood,
They flash upon that inward eye
Which is the bliss of solitude;
And then my heart with pleasure fills,
And dances with the daffodils.

WILLIAM WORDSWORTH

A moment of solace, relishing one of life's simplest pleasures. My favorite chair. And nothing to do. With my knees tucked up underneath my chin and my arms wrapped around my legs, I nestle back to take in the evening's grand display. Before I know it, I am engulfed by the infinite oranges and pinks emblazoned across the sky.

An instant explosion of colors. My soul bursts with joy just to receive this gift of wonder. Can any other moment compare with this one?

As the sun slowly dips beneath the horizon, the moment slips away, leaving behind the distinct sensation that God is near, that He is here.

A little girl reaches for her brother's hand as he walks her home from school. After years of misunderstanding, a friend says, "I'm sorry," restoring the bond once shared. A mother lets go of her son with a kiss on the cheek and watches him climb up those giant school bus steps for the first time. With tears in his eyes and a smile on his face, the father of the bride squeezes his daughter's hand before giving it to her soon-to-be husband. Spelled in different ways, spoken in every language, written and expressed in distinctly personal styles—

love.

No, it is not yours to open buds into blossom.
Shake the bud, strike it,
it is beyond your power to make it blossom....
Oh, it is not for you to open the bud into blossom.
He who can open the bud does it so simply.
He gives it a glance and the life sap
stirs through its veins.
At His breath the flower spreads its wings
and flutters in the wind.
Colors flash out like heart longing,
the perfume betrays a sweet secret.
He who can open the bud does it so simply.

TAGORE

Where can I go from your Spirit?

Where can I flee from your presence?

If I go up to the heavens,

you are there;

if I make my bed in the depths,

you are there.

If I rise on the wings of the dawn,

if I settle on the far side of the sea,

even there your hand will guide me,

your right hand will hold me fast.

PSALM 139:7-10 NIV

God guides us, despite our uncertainties
and our vagueness, even through
our failings and mistakes.... He leads us
step by step, from event to event.
Only afterwards, as we look back over
the way we have come and reconsider certain
moments in our lives in the light of
all that has followed them...
do we experience the feeling of having
been led without knowing it, the feeling
that God has mysteriously guided us.

PAUL TOURNIER

The moments of happiness we enjoy take us by surprise.
It is not that we seize them, but that they seize us.

ASHLEY MONTAGU

It isn't the great big pleasures that count the most;
it's making a great deal out of the little ones.

JEAN WEBSTER

Music I heard with you was more than music,
And bread I broke with you was more than bread.

CONRAD AIKEN

Sometimes I think it is music that binds us
together with harmonies that are part of all
the galaxies and all the stars in their courses.
Music heals, music releases emotions.
Music we hear with each other is indeed more
than music.... Music defies time and separation.
It gives love a melody, memory a tune.
Yes, the music we hear together is more than music.

MADELEINE L'ENGLE

You are special and loved by the One who created you. With each new year of life, may you grow to be as beautiful as He meant you to be when He first thought of you. And may all those around you share in the warmth of the light you carry within.

Light-seeds are planted in the souls of God's people,
Joy-seeds are planted in good heart-soil.

PSALM 97:11 MSG

All the flowers God has made are beautiful.
The rose in its glory and the lily in its whiteness
do not rob the tiny violet of its sweet smell,
or the daisy of its charming simplicity.

ST. THÉRÈSE OF LISIEUX

What a wildly wonderful world, God! You made it all, with Wisdom at your side,
made earth overflow with your wonderful creations.

PSALM 104:24 MSG

Friends are like windows through
which you see out into the world
and back into yourself. Friends.

Friends are like
windows through which
you see out into the

windows through which
dows through which you see out
you see out into the
into the world and back into
world and back into

Today a new sun rises for me; everything lives,
everything is animated, everything seems to speak to me
of my passion, everything invites me to cherish it.

ANNE DE LENCLOS

Is it so small a thing to have enjoyed the sun,
to have lived light in the spring, to have loved,
to have thought, to have done?

MATTHEW ARNOLD

*Love is a fruit in season at all times,
and within the reach of every hand.
Anyone may gather it and no limit is set.*

MOTHER TERESA

*Dear friends, let us love one another,
for love comes from God.*

1 JOHN 4:7 NIV

*J*ust before dawn all is blue: I barely see

the lark bunting light on a fence post.

I stop to admire its white, plump breast,

and for a moment the two of us are alone

in this world, and at peace.

The bunting flies away: white on black

on white on black. Fields to the west are touched

with gold, pale gold with a cast of red....

There is hope, as Miss Dickinson called it,

"the thing with feathers."

There is my soul like a bird.

KATHLEEN NORRIS

Breathing in the clean air of spring, accepting
it as a gift from God.
Fingers in cool wet earth, planting
seeds deep in dirt.
Patiently watching the flowers grow, unfold
their rich color, one petal at a time.
It comes every year—whether we take part
or not—the refreshment of spring,
Renewal and rebirth.

FRIENDS ARE LIKE WINDOWS THROUGH
Friends are like
WHICH YOU SEE OUT INTO THE WORLD
windows through which
AND BACK INTO YOURSELF. FRIENDS
you see out into the
ARE LIKE WINDOWS THROUGH WHICH
world and back into
YOU SEE OUT INTO THE WORLD AND
yourself. Friends are

back into yourself.
INTO THE WORLD AND BACK INTO
Friends are like
YOURSELF. FRIENDS ARE LIKE WIN-
windows through which
DOWS THROUGH WHICH YOU SEE OUT
you see out into the
INTO THE WORLD AND BACK INTO
world and back into
YOURSELF. FRIENDS ARE LIKE

Give generously, for your gifts
will return to you later.

ECCLESIASTES 11:1 TLB

I have found that among its other benefits,

giving liberates the soul of the giver....

When we cast our bread upon the waters, we can

presume that someone downstream whose face

we will never know will benefit from our action,

as we who are downstream from another will

profit from that grantor's gift.

MAYA ANGELOU

*W*ords of encouragement from the heart are priceless in their value. It may be the perfect time for just the words you have to speak, making all the difference in the world to someone. Like a little pebble creates rings rippling out when it is dropped into the water, so a little word of kindness spoken to one heart echoes in another, resounding in heart after heart, setting in motion an ever-widening circle of kindness.

Kind words can be short and easy to speak, but their echoes are truly endless.

MOTHER TERESA

In comparison with this big world,

the human heart is only a small thing.

Though the world is so large,

it is utterly unable to satisfy this tiny heart.

Our ever growing soul and its capacities

can be satisfied only in the infinite God.

As water is restless until it reaches its level,

so the soul has no peace until it rests in God.

SADHU SUNDAR SINGH

Find rest, O my soul, in God alone;
my hope comes from him.

PSALM 62:5 NIV

There is a time for everything,
and a season for every activity under heaven:
a time to be born and a time to die,
a time to plant and a time to uproot...
a time to weep and a time to laugh,
a time to mourn and a time to dance...
a time to love...and a time for peace.
He has made everything beautiful in its time.

ECCLESIASTES 3:1-8,11 NIV

FRIENDS ARE LIKE WINDOWS THROUGH
WHICH YOU SEE OUT INTO THE WORLD
AND BACK INTO YOURSELF. FRIENDS

Friends are like

windows through which

you see out into the

windows through which

DOWS THROUGH WHICH YOU SEE OUT

you see out into the

INTO THE WORLD AND BACK INTO

world and back into

YOURSELF. FRIENDS ARE LIKE

*D*ear Lord, grant me the grace of wonder.

Surprise me, amaze me, awe me in every

crevice of Your universe.... Each day enrapture me

with Your marvelous things without number.

I do not ask to see the reason for it all;

I ask only to share the wonder of it all.

JOSHUA ABRAHAM HESCHEL

Your thoughts—how rare, how beautiful! God, I'll never comprehend them!
I couldn't even begin to count them—any more than I could count
the sands of the sea. Oh, let me rise in the morning and live always with you!

PSALM 139:17-18 MSG

I've written you in thoughts, my friend,
So often through the years,
But somehow ink just couldn't find
The words to make thoughts clear....

I've often written in my thoughts,
But here at last are words
To say I thank you for the joys
That in my heart you've stirred.

CRAIG E. SATHOFF

What is success?

To laugh often and much;

To win the respect of intelligent people

and the affection of children;

To earn the appreciation of honest critics

and endure the betrayal of false friends;

To appreciate beauty;

To find the best in others;

To leave the world a bit better, whether by

a healthy child, a garden patch

or a redeemed social condition;

To know even one life has breathed

easier because you have lived;

This is to have succeeded.

RALPH WALDO EMERSON

Gratitude is the fairest blossom which springs from the soul.

HENRY WARD BEECHER

To be grateful is to recognize the love of God in everything He has given us — and He has given us everything. Every breath we draw is a gift of His love, every moment of existence a gift of grace.

THOMAS MERTON

FRIENDS ARE LIKE WINDOWS THROUGH
Friends are like
WHICH YOU SEE OUT INTO THE WORLD
windows through which
AND BACK INTO YOURSELF. FRIENDS
you see out into the

windows through which
DOWS THROUGH WHICH YOU SEE OUT
you see out into the
INTO THE WORLD AND BACK INTO
world and back into
YOURSELF. FRIENDS ARE LIKE

Eating lunch with a friend. Trying to do a decent day's work. Hearing the rain patter against the window. There is no event so commonplace but that God is present within it, always hiddenly, always leaving you room to recognize Him or not to recognize Him, but all the more fascinatingly because of that, all the more compellingly and hauntingly....

Listen to your life. See it for the fathomless mystery that it is. In the boredom and the pain of it no less than in the excitement and gladness: touch, taste, smell your way to the holy and hidden heart of it because in the last analysis all moments are key moments and life itself is grace.

FREDERICK BUECHNER

The world stands out on either side
No wider than the heart is wide;
Above the world is stretched the sky, —
No higher than the soul is high.
The heart can push the sea and land
Farther away on either hand;
The soul can split the sky in two,
And let the face of God shine through.

EDNA ST. VINCENT MILLAY

Remember running barefoot through the grass,
the wind rushing in your face and the sun shining
warm and bright on your sun-tanned skin?
Days filled with make-believe or hide-and-go-seek.
Hours spent kite-flying or perfecting
"Walk the Dog" with your favorite yo-yo.
Who knew the days of play would disappear so fast?

Even today, play still sets our hearts free
and laughing unwinds the busyness of the day....
To pause for a while, letting moment after moment
of idleness pass by, may be the most efficient use
of my valuable time. To completely lose myself in play
may be the most significant thing I do today.

Lingering in the café, sipping frothy lattes
as their soothing warmth slows us down.
Reveling in these too-brief moments
shared together, we tuck "remember whens"
in between our hurried catching up.
Remember those lazy summer days,
walking through the woods, dreaming together
about what our lives would be? Little do we
know how our hearts are intertwined in an
eternal way—a gift of friendship to
carry us through a lifelong journey.

FRIENDS ARE LIKE WINDOWS THROUGH

Friends are like

WHICH YOU SEE OUT INTO THE WORLD

windows through which

AND BACK INTO YOURSELF. FRIENDS

you see out into the

ARE LIKE WINDOWS THROUGH WHICH

windows through which

DOWS THROUGH WHICH YOU SEE OUT

you see out into the

INTO THE WORLD AND BACK INTO

world and back into

YOURSELF. FRIENDS ARE LIKE

Tender moments of radiant love.
Ignited devotion. Explosions of tenderness...
They remind you about what matters.
A telegram delivered to the back door
of the familiar, telling you to treasure the
treasure you've got while you've got it.
A whisper from an angel, or someone who
sounds like one, reminding you that what
you have is greater than what you want and
that what is urgent is not always what matters.

MAX LUCADO

Hold fast your dreams!
Within your heart
Keep one still, secret spot
Where dreams may go
And, sheltered so,
May thrive and grow.
Where doubt and fear are not.
O keep a place apart,
Within your heart,
For little dreams to go!

LOUISE DRISCOLL

Above all else, guard your heart, for it is the wellspring of life.

PROVERBS 4:23 NIV

Faith is a way of looking at what is seen
and understanding it in a new sense.
Faith is a way of looking at what there
is to be seen in the world and in ourselves and
hoping, trusting, believing against all evidence
to the contrary that beneath the surface we see
there is vastly more that we cannot see....
Faith is the eye of the heart.

FREDERICK BUECHNER

God has put something noble and good into every heart His hand created.

MARK TWAIN

Every single act of love bears the imprint of God.

Friends are like
windows through which
you see out into the
world and back into
yourself. Friends are

back into yourself.
Friends are like
windows through which
you see out into the
world and back into.

It's simple things, like the sound of children playing,
a glowing sunset, or the fresh smell of a meadow that
cause us to pause, marveling with pure wonder and relishing
the simple pleasures of life. Who can hold an autumn leaf
in their hand, or sift the warm white sand on the beach,
and not wonder at the Creator of it all?

Lift your eyes and look to the heavens: Who created all these?
He who brings out the starry host one by one, and calls them each by name....
Do you not know? Have you not heard?
The Lord is the everlasting God, the Creator of the ends of the earth.

ISAIAH 40:26,28 NIV

To know someone here or there with whom you feel there is an understanding in spite of distances or thoughts unexpressed— that can make of this earth a garden.

GOETHE

A friend is one who knows you as you really are, understands where you've been, accepts who you've become, and still gently invites you to grow.

UNKNOWN

Isn't it splendid to think of all the things there are to find out about? It just makes me feel glad to be alive—it's such an interesting world. It wouldn't be half so interesting if we knew all about everything.

LUCY MAUD MONTGOMERY

I still find each day too short for all the thoughts I want to think, all the walks I want to take, all the books I want to read, and all the friends I want to see. The longer I live, the more my mind dwells upon the beauty and the wonder of the world.

JOHN BURROUGHS

My child took a crayon
In her little hand
And started to draw
As if by command....

What are you drawing?
I asked, by and by.
I'm making a picture
Of God in the sky.

But nobody knows
What God looks like, I sighed.
They will when I'm finished
She calmly replied.

SHERWIN KAUFMAN

FRIENDS ARE LIKE WINDOWS THROUGH

Friends are like

WHICH YOU SEE OUT INTO THE WORLD

windows through which

AND BACK INTO YOURSELF. FRIENDS

you see out into the

ARE LIKE WINDOWS THROUGH WHICH

world and back into

YOU SEE OUT INTO THE WORLD AND

yourself. Friends are

back into yourself.

INTO THE WORLD AND BACK INTO

Friends are like

YOURSELF. FRIENDS ARE LIKE WIN

windows through which

DOWS THROUGH WHICH YOU SEE OUT

you see out into the

INTO THE WORLD AND BACK INTO

world and back into

YOURSELF. FRIENDS ARE LIKE

*Write on your heart that every day
is the best day of the year.*

RALPH WALDO EMERSON

Early in the morning, I watch the sun slowly break above the glowing horizon, grateful that today is another chance to start brand new. As I take a pen in hand to write down thoughts and memories in my journal, I realize that today is like this clean white page—a fresh new day stretching out in front of me. May my life be a beautiful script written out on this page of today.

To see a World in a Grain of Sand

And a Heaven in a Wild Flower,

Hold Infinity in the palm of your hand

And Eternity in an hour.

WILLIAM BLAKE

When at last I took the time to look into

the heart of a flower, it opened up a whole new world...

as if a window had been opened to let in the sun.

PRINCESS GRACE OF MONACO

*Sharing with another is a simple
way to say...we need each other.*

JANET L. WEAVER

*We cannot tell the precise moment
when friendship is formed. As in filling
a vessel drop by drop, there is at last
a drop which makes it run over;
so in a series of kindnesses there is at last
one which makes the heart run over.*

SAMUEL JOHNSON

If I had a single flower for every time I think about you, I could walk forever in my garden.

CLAUDIA A. GRANDI